ALICIA KEYS

Gareth Stevens
Publishing

By Molly Shea

Please visit our Web site, www.garethstevens.com. For a free color catalog of all our high-quality books, call toll free 1-800-542-2595 or fax 1-877-542-2596.

Library of Congress Cataloging-in-Publication Data

Shea, Molly.
Alicia Keys / Molly Shea.
    p. cm. — (Hip-hop headliners)
Includes bibliographical references and index.
ISBN 978-1-4339-4784-1 (library binding)
ISBN 978-1-4339-4785-8 (pbk.)
ISBN 978-1-4339-4786-5 (6-pack)
1. Keys, Alicia—Juvenile literature. 2. Singers—United States—Biography—Juvenile literature. I. Title.
ML3930.K39S54 2011
782.42164092—dc22
[B]
                                    2010027404

First Edition

Published in 2011 by
Gareth Stevens Publishing
111 East 14th Street, Suite 349
New York, NY 10003

Copyright © 2011 Gareth Stevens Publishing

Designer: Haley W. Harasymiw
Editor: Therese Shea

Photo credits: Cover, pp. 2–32 (background) Shutterstock.com; cover (Alicia Keys), p. 1 C Flanigan/FilmMagic; p. 5 Martin Rose/Getty Images; pp. 7, 17 Vince Bucci/Getty Images; pp. 9, 15 Frank Micelotta/Getty Images; p. 11 Scott Gries/Image Direct; p. 13 Carlos Alvarez/Getty Images; p. 19 Jason Kempin/Getty Images; p. 21 Peter Kramer/Getty Images; p. 23 STR/AFP/Getty Images; p. 25 Evan Agostini/Getty Images; p. 27 Neil Mockford/ Getty Images; p. 29 Bryan Bedder/Getty Images.

Printed in the United States of America

CPSIA compliance information: Batch #CW11GS: For further information contact Gareth Stevens, New York, New York at 1-800-542-2595.

Contents

Young Alicia   4

Alicia Performing   12

Alicia Writing   20

Alicia Acting   24

Alicia Helping   26

Timeline   30

For More Information   31

Glossary   32

Index   32

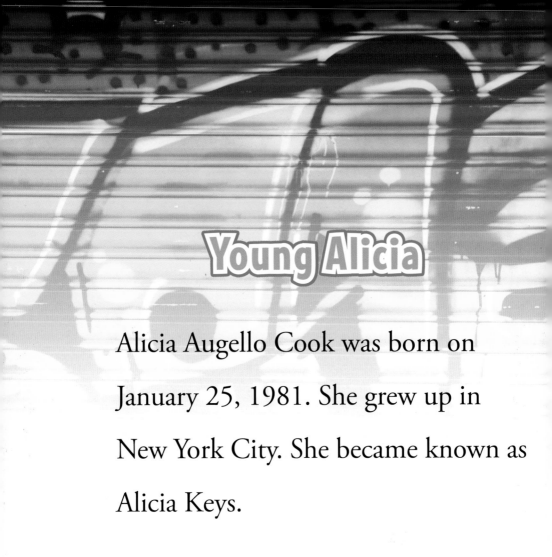

Young Alicia

Alicia Augello Cook was born on January 25, 1981. She grew up in New York City. She became known as Alicia Keys.

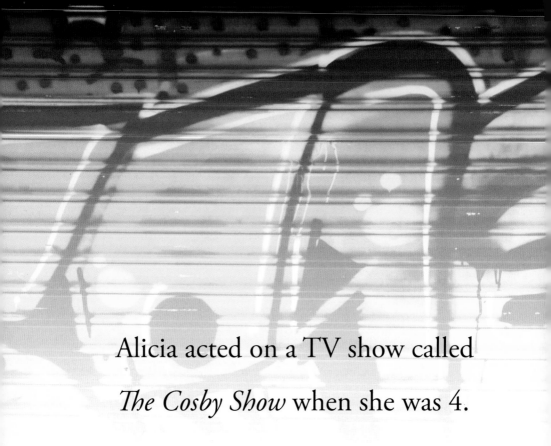

Alicia acted on a TV show called

The Cosby Show when she was 4.

Alicia started playing the piano when she was 7.

Alicia's piano teacher was named
Miss Aziza. Miss Aziza wrote songs.

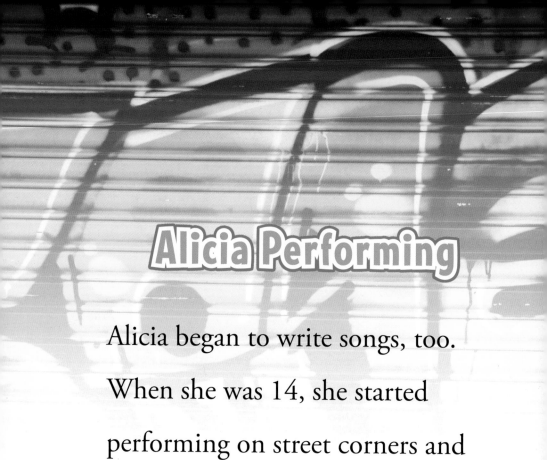

Alicia Performing

Alicia began to write songs, too. When she was 14, she started performing on street corners and in clubs.

Alicia's first album came out in 2001.

She called it *Songs in A Minor*.

"Fallin'" was Alicia's first hit song.
Her album won five Grammys. She
won more for her later albums.

17

Alicia and rapper Jay-Z worked together on a song about New York City. It is called "Empire State of Mind."

Jay-Z

Alicia Writing

Alicia is a writer, too. She named her first book *Tears for Water*. She wrote a book in 2007 called *How Can I Keep From Singing?*

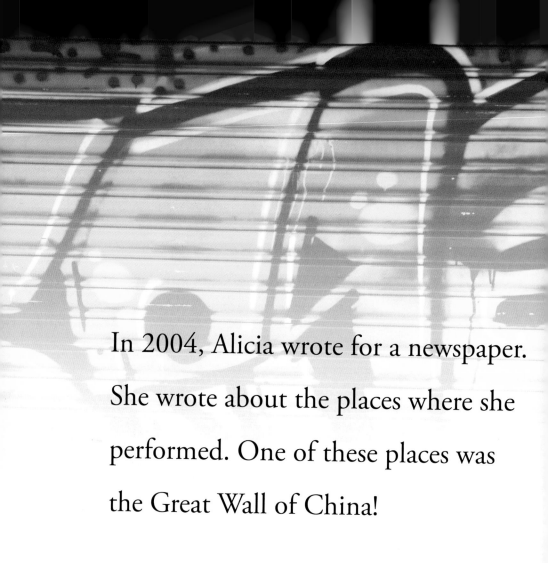

In 2004, Alicia wrote for a newspaper. She wrote about the places where she performed. One of these places was the Great Wall of China!

天下第一雄關

23

Alicia Acting

Alicia has acted in several movies. She acted in *The Secret Life of Bees* and *The Nanny Diaries*.

Alicia Helping

Alicia works with many charities. She helped start a charity called Keep a Child Alive. This charity helps sick children in Africa.

27

Alicia helps young people in
New York City learn about music.
They may grow up to be like her!

Timeline

1981   Alicia Keys is born on January 25 in New York City.

1995   Alicia starts performing on street corners and in clubs.

2001   Alicia's first album comes out.

2002   Alicia helps start Keep a Child Alive.

2004   Alicia's book *Tears for Water* comes out.

2008   The movie *The Secret Life of Bees* comes out.

2009   Alicia and Jay-Z's "Empire State of Mind" comes out.

For More Information

Books:

Brown, Terrell. *Alicia Keys*. Broomall, PA: Mason Crest
Publishers, 2007.

Roberts, Russell. *Alicia Keys*. Broomall, PA: Mason Crest
Publishers, 2010.

Web Sites:

Alicia Keys
www.aliciakeys.com

Alicia Keys
www.imdb.com/name/nm1006024/

Keep a Child Alive
keepachildalive.org

Publisher's note to educators and parents: Our editors have carefully reviewed these Web sites to ensure that
they are suitable for students. Many Web sites change frequently, however, and we cannot guarantee that a site's
future contents will continue to meet our high standards of quality and educational value. Be advised that students
should be closely supervised whenever they access the Internet.

Glossary

A minor: a certain sound in music

charity: a group that helps people in need

club: a place with music and dancing

Grammy: an honor given to someone for their music

perform: to sing or play music

Index

act 6, 24
book 20, 30
charities 26
clubs 12, 30
Cook, Alicia Augello 4
Cosby Show, The 6
"Empire State of Mind" 18, 30
"Fallin' " 16

Grammys 16
Great Wall of China 22
How Can I Keep From Singing? 20
Jay-Z 18, 19, 30
Keep a Child Alive 26, 30
Miss Aziza 10
Nanny Diaries, The 24
newspaper 22

New York City 4, 18, 28, 30
piano 8, 10
Secret Life of Bees, The 24, 30
songs 10, 12, 16, 18
Songs in A Minor 14
street corners 12, 30
Tears for Water 20, 30
writer 20